Wonders of the World

Amazon Rain Forest

Galadriel Watson

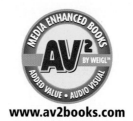

www.av2books.com

AV² provides enriched content that supplements and complements this book. Weigl's AV² books strive to create inspired learning and engage young minds in a total learning experience.

Your AV² Media Enhanced books come alive with...

Audio
Listen to sections of the book read aloud.

Key Words
Study vocabulary, and complete a matching word activity.

Video
Watch informative video clips.

Quizzes
Test your knowledge.

Embedded Weblinks
Gain additional information for research.

Slide Show
View images and captions, and prepare a presentation.

Try This!
Complete activities and hands-on experiments.

... and much, much more!

Go to **www.av2books.com**, and enter this book's unique code.

BOOK CODE

T 3 9 7 8 7 4

AV² by Weigl brings you media enhanced books that support active learning.

Published by AV² by Weigl
350 5th Avenue, 59th Floor
New York, NY 10118
Website: www.av2books.com   www.weigl.com

Copyright ©2013 AV² by Weigl
All rights reserved. No part of this publication may be reproduced, stored in a retrieval system, or transmitted in any form or by any means, electronic, mechanical, photocopying, recording, or otherwise, without the prior written permission of the publisher.

Library of Congress Cataloging-in-Publication Data

Watson, Galadriel Findlay.
Amazon rain forest / Galadriel Watson.
     p. cm. -- (Wonders of the world)
Includes index.
ISBN 978-1-61913-522-2 (hard cover : alk. paper) -- ISBN 978-1-61913-435-5 (soft cover : alk. paper) -- ISBN 978-1-61913-553-6 (ebook)
 1. Amazon River Region--Juvenile literature. I. Title.
F2546.W29 2012
981'.1--dc23
                          2012010884

Printed in the United States of America in North Mankato, Minnesota
3 4 5 6 7 8 9 17 16 15 14 13

042013
WEP170413

Project Coordinator Heather Kissock
Design Mandy Christiansen

Every reasonable effort has been made to trace ownership and to obtain permission to reprint copyright material. The publishers would be pleased to have any errors or omissions brought to their attention so that they may be corrected in subsequent printings.

Photo Credits
Weigl acknowledges Getty Images and Alamy as primary photo suppliers for this title.

Contents

A Wealth of Life

With an area of more than 2 million square miles (5.2 million square kilometers), the Amazon rain forest in South America is the largest rain forest in the world. It is so large that it covers an area equal to about half of the United States.

A wealth of plants and animals live in this vast region. In fact, more **species** of plants and animals live in the Amazon rain forest than in any other place on Earth. Fruits, nuts, coffee, and other foods are farmed in the Amazon. Certain plants are used to make important medicines. Thousands of types of monkeys, birds, insects, and other animals thrive in the rain forest's hot, wet climate.

Many plant and animal species in the rain forest have yet to be identified.

Macaws feed on tropical nuts and fruits. While scarlet macaws are still frequently seen in the Amazon canopy, their numbers are declining.

Amazon Rain Forest Facts

- Temperatures in the Amazon rain forest average about 80° Fahrenheit (27° Celsius), with up to 90 percent humidity. To humans, this feels like a steam bath.

- The Amazon region receives about 9 feet (2.7 meters) of rainfall per year. By comparison, the average U.S. city receives less than 3 feet (0.9 m) per year.

- The Amazon rain forest covers about one-third of the continent of South America.

- The rain forest surrounds the Amazon River, which is the second-longest river in the world. The Nile in Africa is the longest river in the world.

- The Amazon River carries 16 percent of the global river flow.

- The equator runs across the northern portion of the Amazon rain forest. Almost all of the world's tropical rain forests are located on or near the equator.

Map of the Amazon Rain Forest

Equator

Gulf of
Guayaquil

AMAZON RAIN FOREST

*Atlantic
Ocean*

South America

*Pacific
Ocean*

Gulf of San Matias

*Gulf of
San Jorge*

Strait of Magellan

Legend

Amazon Rain Forest

---- International border

N
W · E
S

Scale

0   500 Miles

0   500 Kilometers

Where in the World?

The Amazon rain forest is home to the 4,000-mile (6,437-km) Amazon River. It runs from the Andes Mountains to the Atlantic Ocean on the east coast of South America. Along the way, more than 1,000 **tributaries** feed into the Amazon. When the warm season arrives in the Andes, mountain snowmelt runs down to the Amazon. The already huge river swells and floods.

Squirrel monkeys use their long tails for balance as they climb from limb to limb in the Amazon rain forest.

The Amazon rain forest surrounds the river. Much of the region is wild jungle, and few cities exist there. Part of the rain forest sits in the Tumucumaque Mountains National Park in Brazil. This protected area is the largest tropical forest national park in the world.

The twisting, winding route of the Amazon River crosses nine different South American countries. During the rainy season, the river's width can reach 120 miles (190 km).

Puzzler

Most of the Amazon rain forest lies in the country of Brazil, but it also extends into eight other countries.

Q: Identify each of the countries on the map.

HINT: This country has more oil reserves than any other country in the Americas and is home to the largest lake in South America.

HINT: This country has coasts on both the Caribbean Sea and the Pacific Ocean.

HINT: This is the smallest country in South America and its official language is Dutch.

HINT: This country is an overseas department of France.

HINT: This country owns the Galapagos Islands.

HINT: Originally settled by the Dutch, this country won its independence from Britain in 1966.

HINT: Lake Titicaca and the ruins of Machu Picchu are located in this country.

HINT: This is the largest country in South America.

HINT: La Paz, this country's administrative capital, is the highest capital city in the world.

Pacific Ocean

Atlantic Ocean

A: A. Peru   B. Ecuador   C. Columbia   D. Venezuela   E. Guyana   F. Suriname   G. French Guiana   H. Brazil   I. Bolivia

A Trip Back in Time

Millions of years ago, before humans lived on Earth, the Amazon River flowed west into the Pacific Ocean. Later, the region's tectonic plates, the rigid pieces of land that make up Earth's outer shell, began to shift. The tectonic shift pushed up huge masses of rock to form the Andes Mountains. With the mountains in its path, the Amazon River gradually found a new route. Eventually, the river moved east and reached the Atlantic Ocean. This change occurred about 8 million years ago.

In some parts of the world, such as North America, **ice age** glaciers covered the land and killed most living things. The Amazon, however, has never been covered by glaciers. This has allowed Amazon plant and animal species to develop uninterrupted for millions of years.

Like the rain forest itself, many Amazon trees are very old. Some ceiba trees have been known to live for more than two centuries.

Rain Forest Layers

The rain forest is divided into several layers, each with very different living conditions.

Emergents: Gigantic treetops rise above the rest of the forest's trees. Mostly birds and insects live here. This layer receives more sunlight than other layers.

Canopy: The treetops reach up to 165 feet (50 m). This area traps the most water and sunlight. These treetops produce the most food for the forest's creatures.

Understory: Here live shorter, younger trees that reach to about 60 feet (18 m). Only about 2 percent of sunlight reaches the understory.

Floor: The floor is dark. Only 0–2 percent of sunlight and very little water reach the floor. Few plants can grow in this darkness. The ground is covered with a layer of decomposing leaves and other matter called **humus**. Many fungi and insects live on the floor layer.

Plentiful Plants

Only a small amount of light and water reach the floor of the rain forest, so the soil is too poor to allow many plants to grow in the ground. In other environments, plants draw **nutrients** from the soil, but rain forest plants keep most nutrients in their leaves and tissues. They also receive nutrients from the floor's layer of humus.

Despite the poor soil, the Amazon rain forest holds countless types of plants. There are more than 2,500 species of trees. Many other plants make their homes in these trees. Lianas—thick, woody vines—connect to young trees in the understory. They grow upward and attach themselves to taller branches. Some lianas grow as high as the canopy.

Epiphytes, also called "air plants," do not have roots in the soil. They live above ground, attached to other plants. They do not feed off their host plant, but rather draw nutrients from air and rain.

The Rainy Season

The rain forest has two seasons, a rainy season and a dry season. The rainy season in the Amazon lasts about four months. There is still plenty of sunshine, but the clouds take every opportunity to release huge amounts of water. Also, during the rainy season, water from snow melting in the Andes runs down the mountains and flows into rivers and streams. Together, the rain and melted snow make for massive flooding in the rain forest. Vast areas of the forest floor are covered in water. Animals either climb trees or scramble to seek higher ground.

The dry season of the Amazon is still quite wet, but the rain is far less frequent. The floodwaters recede, allowing animals to return to the flooded land.

Rainy-season downpours can be so heavy that 1 or 2 inches (2.5 to 5 centimeters) of rain can fall in just one hour.

Amazon Animals

Some incredible creatures live in the Amazon rain forest. Animals must be on guard against the anaconda, a huge water snake that kills its prey by wrapping its body around the other animal and squeezing it to death. One of the largest spiders in the world, the 10-inch (25-cm) bird-eating spider, lives in the Amazon, too. There are also many mammals, such as sloths, monkeys, and the vampire bat.

Scientists may never know exactly how many animals live in the Amazon. They estimate that there are 1,500 bird species, 3,000 fish species, and 500 mammal species. Rain forest scientists often identify animal species that have never been known to humans.

In the last decade, more than 1,200 new species have been discovered in the Amazon region, and that number does not include insects. Thirty-nine of these new species are mammals. They include a pink river dolphin and, most recently, two new species of monkeys.

Owl butterflies are big. Their wingspan can be up to 8 inches (20 cm), making them one of the largest butterfly species in the Amazon rain forest. The eyespots on their wings are used to either redirect attacks from their bodies to their wings or to scare other animals away.

Endangered Species

Some scientists estimate that about 100 plant and animal species become extinct every day in the world's rain forests. This means if the last member of the species dies, the species will never return to life again. Extinction is caused by changes in the rain forest ecosystem. Some causes are natural. Others are caused by humans.

The Amazon's jaguar population is currently in danger. Local ranchers kill jaguars if they suspect the cats have been attacking their herds. Hunters also kill jaguars for their fur.

A threatened plant species is the mahogany tree. People around the world love furniture made of the dark reddish-brown mahogany wood. The trees are cut down so frequently that mahogany might soon become extinct in the Amazon.

The jaguar makes its home in the trees of the rain forest. When trees are cut down, the jaguar's habitat is destroyed.

Researching the Forest

The Amazon rain forest canopy holds many mysteries. Since the canopy is so hard to reach, scientists have studied it less than the ocean floor.

In the 1800s, European explorers hired **indigenous** peoples to climb the trees and bring down samples of plant life. Presently, scientists can measure trees using **lasers**. They also use **satellite** pictures to study large areas of the forest. In recent years, scientists have built platforms high in the trees so they can get a closeup look at canopy life. One scientist even developed a canopy "raft," a large platform that floats in the air. It is held up by helium-filled tubes.

Walkways allow people to travel through the canopy of the rain forest on foot. Walkways lead to platforms, where people can stay for hours, or even camp for days.

Henry Walter Bates (1825–1892)

Henry Walter Bates spent more than a decade studying nature in the Amazon rain forest. Bates was a naturalist, a scientist who studies nature. He was the first person to identify about 7,000 rain forest insects. Bates described his findings in his book, *The Naturalist on the River Amazons*, which was published in 1863.

Bates was well known for his studies on insect mimicry. Mimicry is when a species of animal looks like another species so that **predators** cannot easily see the animal. For example, the viceroy butterfly, which is eaten by birds, looks like the monarch butterfly, which birds hate to eat. Since the viceroy looks like the monarch, birds often leave the viceroy alone. This animal trait is called "Batesian mimicry," named after Bates.

Bates' book shows him exploring the Amazon basin.

Facts of Life

Born: February 8, 1825

Hometown: Leicester, England

Occupation: Naturalist

Died: February 16, 1892

The Big Picture

The Amazon rain forest is one of several rain forests in the world. The largest rain forests are in Central and South America, Asia, and Africa. Although these forests cover only about 7 percent of Earth's land, they are home to more than 50 percent of its plant and animal species.

Maya Biosphere Reserve
Guatemala, Central America

Amazon Rain Forest
South America

NORTH AMERICA

ATLANTIC OCEAN

EQUATOR

PACIFIC OCEAN

SOUTH AMERICA

SOUTHERN OCEAN

Legend

☐	Ocean
☐	Rain forest

Scale at Equator

0   1,000   2,000   3,000 miles

0   1,000   2,000   3,000 kilometers

N
W   E
S

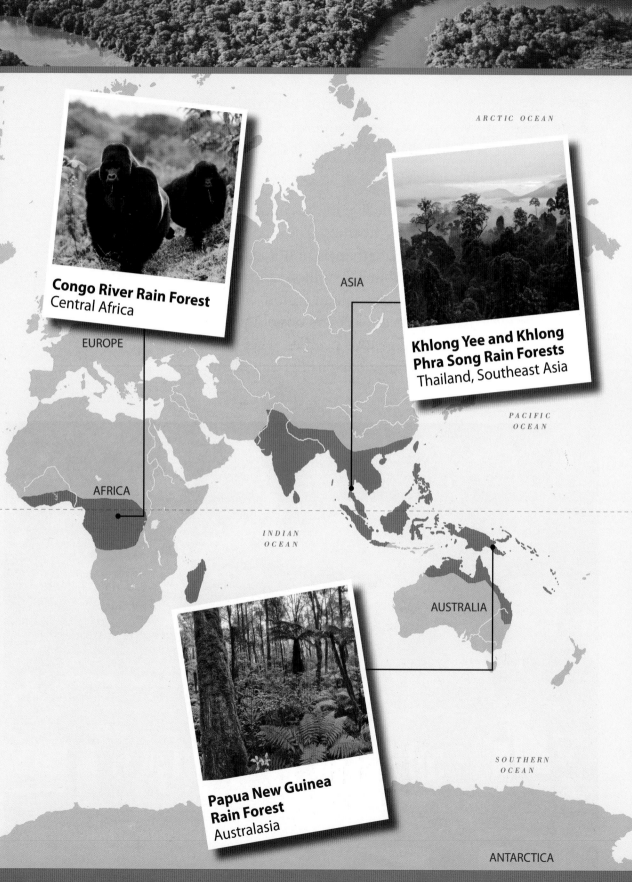

Congo River Rain Forest
Central Africa

**Khlong Yee and Khlong
Phra Song Rain Forests**
Thailand, Southeast Asia

**Papua New Guinea
Rain Forest**
Australasia

ARCTIC OCEAN

ASIA

EUROPE

AFRICA

PACIFIC
OCEAN

INDIAN
OCEAN

AUSTRALIA

SOUTHERN
OCEAN

ANTARCTICA

People of the Amazon

The first people to live in the Amazon arrived thousands of years ago. When Spanish conquerors called conquistadors arrived in the 1500s, they destroyed many of these ancient civilizations.

Today, about 20 million people live in the Amazon region. About half of these people live in cities. The city of Manaus, Brazil, has a population of more than 1.5 million. The city of Belém has a population of about 1.7 million, and well over 2 million live in the Belém metropolitan region. Many other people of the Amazon region are farmers or gold prospectors. Only about 250,000 are indigenous peoples. They belong to more than 150 ethnic groups, such as the Yanomami, the Xikrin, and the Juruna.

Amazon rain forest families build their homes on stilts so they can stay above water during the rainy season.

Puzzler

Since the Amazon rain forest is crisscrossed with waterways, and because so much of it floods during the rainy season, the best way to travel is by boat. Native peoples still make their own, just as they have for centuries.

Q: From what material are the Amazon canoes called *pirogues* made?

A: These boats are made from hollowed tree trunks.

Timeline

90 million years ago

The Andes Mountains begin to form.

30 million years ago

The Amazon River is cut off from the Pacific Ocean.

8 million years ago

The Amazon River breaks through to the Atlantic Ocean.

10,000–15,000 years ago

The Amazon's earliest inhabitants arrive.

1500s

European explorers first arrive in the Amazon basin.

1500s

The Spanish conquistadors destroy entire indigenous civilizations.

1541

Europeans complete their first trip down the entire length of the Amazon River.

1740s

Europeans in the Amazon discover **latex**, which becomes a key substance in producing rubber and plastic products.

1848

Henry Walter Bates first travels to the Amazon.

1863

Henry Walter Bates publishes his book *The Naturalist on the River Amazons*.

1892

Henry Walter Bates dies.

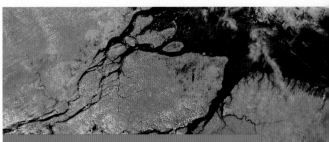

8 million years ago The Amazon River begins to flow into the Atlantic Ocean.

1850s Bates discovers a wealth of exotic plants in the Amazon basin.

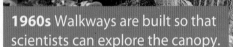

1960s Walkways are built so that scientists can explore the canopy.

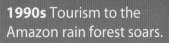

1990s Tourism to the Amazon rain forest soars.

2000s Severe droughts wreak havoc on the people of the Amazon.

2000s Forest fires rage out of control.

2010s Scientists continue to discover new species of animals.

1950

The world's rain forests cover about 8,700,000 square miles (22,532,896 sq km).

1960s

Researchers build the first suspended walkways in the rain forest.

1970s

Researchers use mountain-climbing equipment to pull themselves up to the canopy.

1980s

After studying insect life in the Amazon, a researcher determines there are up to 30 million insect species in the world.

1989

The canopy raft is invented.

2002

Brazil's portion of the Amazon loses 10,000 square miles (25,900 sq km) to **deforestation**.

2002

The Brazilian government announces the creation of Tumucumaque Mountains National Park.

2005

The Amazon experiences a severe drought. Thousands of square miles (km) burn.

2010

A new species of long-tailed monkey is discovered in Mato Grosso, Brazil.

The Disappearing Forest

The Amazon rain forest is disappearing at an alarming rate. In 2011, nearly 1,000 square miles (2,408 sq km) of rain forest were cut or burned just in Brazil. This is less than losses in preceding years. However, since 2005, more than 8,800 square miles (23,000 sq km) of the forest have disappeared. This area is about the same size as the state of Massachusetts. Deforestation is a difficult issue because there are both good and bad reasons to clear trees. For instance, the wood from these trees makes products such as furniture and flooring. This brings money into the area economies. On the other hand, deforestation destroys some animals' habitats.

Rain forest trees are cleared to make way for new farms and ranches, to create roads, and to reach mines.

Governments and businesses try to replace some of the deforested areas. However, the ecosystems that grow in these newer forests contain fewer plant and animal species. Once an ancient rain forest area is cleared, it is likely gone forever.

Should trees be cut down in the Amazon rain forest?

Yes	No
The world's population is increasing and needs wood for fuel and timber.	Countless plant and animal species are wiped out by deforestation.
Selling rain forest trees brings much-needed income into the region.	Indigenous peoples lose their homes and eventually forget important knowledge about the land, its species, and its history.
Land needs to be cleared to build new settlements so people can move out of overcrowded cities.	The loss of trees causes local air temperatures to rise, reduces the amount of rain in the area, and increases the level of **carbon dioxide** in the atmosphere. These factors all contribute to the **greenhouse effect**.

Natural Attractions

Tourists who visit the Amazon rain forest are vital to its survival for many reasons. Perhaps most importantly, tourism brings money to people who have little. Visitors spend money on hotels, food, and local products. Also, tourism encourages the local inhabitants to properly care for the wilderness so it will continue to attract visitors. Some hotels have built walkways and platforms to allow tourists to observe the canopy ecosystem just as scientists are able to do.

The vast rain forest offers visitors many different opportunities for exploration. Some people travel to the Meeting of the Waters, a place where the dark and light waters of two rivers run side-by-side without mixing. Others visit Lake Janauari Ecological Park to see giant water lilies, measuring up to 7 feet (2.1 m) across.

Tour companies lead visitors on boat tours through the rain forest. Tourists can also hire guides to take them hiking through parts of the forest floor.

Be Prepared

A visit to the Amazon rain forest can be a rough and rugged trip, but with proper preparation, it can be safe, fascinating, and the experience of a lifetime.

It is important to dress for very hot temperatures and high humidity. Loose-fitting cotton clothing is best.

If traveling on foot through the forest floor, some tour companies recommend bringing "mud shoes," an old pair of inexpensive sneakers.

Many areas of the forest floor receive little sunlight even during daytime, so a flashlight will help in the dark.

Since most of the animals reside high in the canopy, a pair of binoculars is the best way to see them.

A rain forest visit will not be spent entirely in the shade. Be prepared for sunny spots by bringing sunscreen, a hat, and sunglasses.

Be sure to bring insect repellent.

Heavy rains can occur at anytime, so a good raincoat or poncho is needed.

Visitors should always have a camera ready. Tourists cannot take plants or animals home from the rain forest, but they can take as many pictures as they want.

Local Knowledge

O ver the thousands of years that indigenous peoples have lived in the Amazon, they have come to know many of the plants and their uses. Some of this knowledge has spread to other parts of the world.

For example, Brazil nuts, pineapples, and cocoa are popular foods from the Amazon region. Rubber taken from the Amazon's rubber trees is used in many places around the world, as well. *Guaraná* is a drink made from an Amazonian seed that has up to five times more **caffeine** than coffee. Doctors treat the disease malaria with a medicine called quinine, which comes from the bark of the Amazon's cinchona tree. Drug companies around the world use many other key ingredients from Amazon plants to make important, life-saving medicines.

Indigenous people rely on native plants for both food and medicine. Many types of mushrooms are poisonous, but the Yanomami people have learned which species are safe to eat and which are not.

Amazon Mythology

Manioc is another name for cassava, a starchy root used to make flour. According to local mythology, manioc has magical beginnings. The legend says that long ago, the daughter of a Native chieftain gave birth to a beautiful boy, whom she named Mani. Mani was loved very much, but he died at three years of age. Mani's mother buried him near her house and wept over his grave. Eventually, a plant began to grow from the grave. The plant was named manioc, after the little boy Mani.

Manioc plants grow in the Amazon rain forest. The food is in the root of the plant, which is buried underground.

True or False?

Decide whether the following statements are true or false. If the statement is false, make it true.

1. Henry Walter Bates was a conquistador.

2. According to legend, manioc is named after a boy named Mani.

3. People know much more about the rain forest canopy than the ocean floor.

4. The Amazon's jaguar population is increasing.

5. Humus is made partly of decomposing leaves.

6. Income from tourism encourages local people to take care of the Amazon wilderness.

ANSWERS
1. False. He was a naturalist.
2. True
3. False. They know less about the canopy.
4. False. The jaguar population is decreasing.
5. True
6. True

Short Answer

Answer the following questions using information from the book.

1. To what ocean does the Amazon River flow?
2. What did not cover the Amazon during an ice age?
3. What are the names of the rain forest's layers?
4. What kind of plant does not need soil?
5. What drink has more caffeine than coffee?

ANSWERS
1. The Atlantic Ocean
2. Glaciers
3. Emergents, Canopy, Understory, Floor
4. An epiphyte, or "air plant"
5. Guaraná

Multiple Choice

Choose the best answer for the following questions.

1. The Amazon rain forest is mostly in:
    a. Mexico
    b. Brazil
    c. Ecuador
    d. Argentina

2. Pirogues are a type of:
    a. Food
    b. Flower
    c. Fish
    d. Boat

3. What group of indigenous peoples lives in the Amazon?
    a. The Yanomami
    b. The San
    c. The Aztecs
    d. The Mohawks

4. What do doctors use as a treatment for malaria?
    a. Brazil nut
    b. guaraná
    c. curare
    d. quinine

1.b 2.d 3.a 4.d

ANSWERS

Rubber from the Rain forest

About 60,000 families make their living tapping rubber trees in the Amazon rain forest. Rubber comes from a milky white substance inside the trees. Tapping them does not kill the tree, and a rubber tree can be tapped for about 20 years. Try this experiment to make your own rubber-like material.

Materials

Rubber gloves

Borax powder

Measuring cup

Measuring spoons

White glue

Popsicle stick

Instructions

1 Put on rubber or latex gloves to protect your hands.

2 Mix 1 cup (237 ml) of water with 1 tablespoon (15 ml) of borax.

3 In a separate plastic container, thoroughly mix 1-2/3 tablespoons (25 ml) of white glue, with 1-1/3 tablespoons (20 ml) of water.

4 Add 1 teaspoon (5 ml) of the borax solution into the glue-and-water mixture. Stir with the wooden coffee stirrer or Popsicle stick. When a solid substance has adhered to the stirrer, peel it off and knead it onto a paper towel until it loses its stickiness.

Results

A rubbery material will be formed. It will have the consistency of putty. Try stretching it. Form it into a ball, and bounce it. Think about the many daily uses for rubber, at home, at school, and in industries around the world.

Key Words

caffeine: a substance in plants such as coffee and tea that, when consumed, can make people feel alert

carbon dioxide: a gas that is found normally in the atmosphere and is absorbed by plants

deforestation: the act of removing trees from an area

greenhouse effect: the dangerous warming of Earth

humus: a brownish, mushy substance made up of dead, decomposing parts of plants and animal waste on a forest floor

ice age: a period of time when a large area of Earth is covered by glaciers

indigenous: native to a certain place; having been born in a place

lasers: devices that emit a beam of radiation

latex: a liquid produced by certain types of plants that is made into rubber

nutrients: any substance that provides nourishment when consumed

predators: animals that hunt and kill other animals for food

satellite: a spacecraft that travels around Earth and transmits communication signals

species: a specific group of plants or animals that shares characteristics

tributaries: bodies of water that feed into larger bodies of water, such as rivers

Index

Log on to www.av2books.com

AV² by Weigl brings you media enhanced books that support active learning. Go to www.av2books.com, and enter the special code found on page 2 of this book. You will gain access to enriched and enhanced content that supplements and complements this book. Content includes video, audio, weblinks, quizzes, a slide show, and activities.

Audio
Listen to sections of the book read aloud.

Video
Watch informative video clips.

Embedded Weblinks
Gain additional information for research.

Try This!
Complete activities and hands-on experiments.

WHAT'S ONLINE?

Try This!	Embedded Weblinks	Video	EXTRA FEATURES
Map where the Amazon rain forest is and the features that surround it.	Learn more about the Amazon rain forest.	Take a flight over the Amazon rain forest.	**Audio** Listen to sections of the book read aloud.
Write a biography of an explorer who traveled the Amazon rain forest.	Play games related to the Amazon rain forest.	Watch this video to learn more about the issues facing the Amazon rain forest.	**Key Words** Study vocabulary, and complete a matching word activity.
Locate major rain forests around the world.	Find out more about early explorers of the Amazon rain forest.		**Slide Show** View images and captions, and prepare a presentation.
Complete a timeline that outlines the history of the Amazon rain forest.			
Test your knowledge of the Amazon rain forest.			**Quizzes** Test your knowledge.

AV² was built to bridge the gap between print and digital. We encourage you to tell us what you like and what you want to see in the future.

Sign up to be an AV² Ambassador at www.av2books.com/ambassador.

Due to the dynamic nature of the Internet, some of the URLs and activities provided as part of AV² by Weigl may have changed or ceased to exist. AV² by Weigl accepts no responsibility for any such changes. All media enhanced books are regularly monitored to update addresses and sites in a timely manner. Contact AV² by Weigl at 1-866-649-3445 or av2books@weigl.com with any questions, comments, or feedback.

P9-DMH-085